Language Arts 1 Copywork

Easy Peasy

All-in-One
Homeschool

This is just the copywork from Language Arts 1 of Easy Peasy All-in-One Homeschool.

This was created for the sake of convenience. Where in the online course it says to copy certain words or sentences, those have been included here. I hope this helps your family.

Lesson 2

His wife shuddered.

_____

_____

_____

_____

_____

_____

Lesson 4

So Jolly Robin thanked him.

_____

_____

_____

_____

_____

_____

Lesson 6

The struggle was over in a moment.

_____

_____

_____

_____

_____

_____

Lesson 7

On some days there was no sun
at all.

_____

_____

_____

_____

_____

_____

Lesson 8

His wife, however, shook her head.

_____

_____

_____

_____

_____

_____

Lesson 9

He had expected to have a ride.

_____

_____

_____

_____

_____

_____

Lesson 11

And Jolly Robin did not laugh.

_____

_____

_____

_____

_____

_____

Lesson 13

I'd like to hear you sing!

_____

_____

_____

_____

_____

_____

Lesson 14

And so all the weeping he might do would be merely wasted.

_____

_____

_____

_____

_____

_____

Lesson 15

His cousin shook his head at that.

_____

_____

_____

_____

_____

_____

Lesson 16

The feathered folk in Pleasant Valley were all aflutter.

_____

_____

_____

_____

_____

_____

Lesson 17

But all the others gazed at him in
amazement.

_____

_____

_____

_____

_____

_____

Lesson 18

Several times Jasper tried.

_____

_____

_____

_____

_____

_____

Lesson 19

Mr. Crow looked up quickly.

_____

_____

_____

_____

_____

_____

_____

Lesson 20

Mr. Crow was more than willing.

_____

_____

_____

_____

_____

_____

Lesson 31

That was unfortunate for the mice.

_____

_____

_____

_____

_____

_____

Lesson 32

It was really a good thing for
Solomon Owl.

_____

_____

_____

_____

_____

_____

Lesson 37

Then Solomon sat up and listened.

_____

_____

_____

_____

_____

_____

_____

Lesson 40

"What have you been eating?" she inquired.

_____

_____

_____

_____

_____

_____

Lesson 41

"Good!" she exclaimed with a smile.

_____

_____

_____

_____

_____

_____

Lesson 42

It was different with Benjamin Bat.

_____

_____

_____

_____

_____

_____

Lesson 44

"What makes you think that?" Benjamin Bat inquired.

_____

_____

_____

_____

_____

_____

Lesson 45

"Oh, I shall be willing to step outside," Solomon told him.

_____

_____

_____

_____

_____

_____

Lesson 47

"You surely ought to be glad to please your own cousin," he told Simon.

_____

_____

_____

_____

_____

_____

Lesson 86

Jolly Robin's worrying wife wouldn't give him a moment's peace.

_____

_____

_____

_____

_____

_____

Lesson 87

Jolly Robin told his wife how he swooped down over Reddy Woodpecker's head.

_____

_____

_____

_____

_____

_____

Lesson 89

One day Reddy Woodpecker was tap, tap, tapping on a tall poplar that grew beside the brook.

_____

_____

_____

_____

_____

_____

Lesson 97

Reddy Woodpecker had no patience with him.

_____

_____

_____

_____

_____

_____

Lesson 98

It's no wonder Reddy was angry.

_____

_____

_____

_____

_____

_____

Lesson 99

Then Frisky sat up on a limb and glared at him.

_____

_____

_____

_____

_____

_____

Lesson 100

Frisky did not intend to go hungry when winter came.

_____

_____

_____

_____

_____

_____

Lesson 106

No, it wasn't that.

_____

_____

_____

_____

_____

_____

Lesson 107

Old Mr. Toad just laughed.

_____

_____

_____

_____

_____

_____

Lesson 108

By and by he turned his head.

_____

_____

_____

_____

_____

_____

Lesson 110

"Next time I'll get him!"

_____

_____

_____

_____

_____

_____

_____

Lesson 111

ship shop shape shine shirt shoe

_____

_____

_____

_____

_____

_____

Lesson 112

"That's good," said she.

_____

_____

_____

_____

_____

_____

Lesson 116

chin chip chop cheap
church churn

Lesson 119

So Peter hurried over to the nearest tree.

_____

_____

_____

_____

_____

_____

Lesson 121

who what why where when which

_____

_____

_____

_____

_____

_____

Lesson 123

By and by, happening to look across the snow-covered Green Meadows, he saw something that made his heart jump.

_____

_____

_____

_____

_____

Lesson 124

Peter Rabbit sat in his secretest place in the dear Old Briar-patch.

_____

_____

_____

_____

_____

_____

_____

Lesson 126

this that they thing think there

_____

_____

_____

_____

_____

_____

Lesson 134

this thing where why shop shoe
chop church

_____

_____

_____

_____

_____

_____

Lesson 136

bikes stores cars tables friends
times

_____

_____

_____

_____

_____

_____

Lesson 137

washes misses brushes peaches
wishes taxes

_____

_____

_____

_____

_____

_____

Lesson 138

toys ways days plays keys

_____

_____

_____

_____

_____

_____

Lesson 141

Who makes an enemy a friend, to fear and worry puts an end.

_____

_____

_____

_____

_____

_____

_____

Lesson 142

There the same thing happened.

_____

_____

_____

_____

_____

_____

Lesson 143

A sudden odd surprise made Farmer Brown's boy's hair to rise.

_____

_____

_____

_____

_____

_____

Lesson 144

"What is it?"

_____

_____

_____

_____

_____

_____

Lesson 145

"That's a splendid idea!"

_____

_____

_____

_____

_____

_____

Lesson 146

shelves knives loaves wolves
leaves

_____

_____

_____

_____

_____

_____

Lesson 150

My favorite place to be is

_____

_____

_____

_____

_____

_____

Lesson 163

All things bright and beautiful

_____

_____

_____

_____

_____

_____

Lesson 164

All creatures great and small

_____

_____

_____

_____

_____

_____

Lesson 165

All things wise and wonderful

_____

_____

_____

_____

_____

_____

Lesson 166

The Lord God made them all.

_____

_____

_____

_____

_____

_____

Lesson 167

He gave us eyes to see them,

_____

_____

_____

_____

_____

_____

Lesson 168

And lips that we might tell

_____

_____

_____

_____

_____

_____

Lesson 169

How great is God Almighty,

_____

_____

_____

_____

_____

_____

Lesson 170

Who has made all things well.

_____

_____

_____

_____

_____

_____

The Easy Peasy All-in-One Homeschool is a free, complete online homeschool curriculum. There are 180 days of ready-to-go assignments for every level and every subject. It's created for your children to work as independently as you want them to. Preschool through high school is available as well as courses ranging from English, math, science and history to art, music, computer, thinking, physical education and health. A daily Bible lesson is offered as well. The mission of Easy Peasy is to enable those to homeschool who otherwise thought they couldn't.

The Genesis Curriculum takes the Bible and turns it into lessons for your homeschool. Daily lessons include Bible reading, memory verse, spelling, handwriting, vocabulary, grammar, Biblical language, science, social studies, writing, and thinking through discussion questions.

The Genesis Curriculum uses a complete book of the Bible for one full year. The curriculum is being made using both Old and New Testament books. Find us online at genesiscurriculum.com to read about the latest developments in this expanding curriculum.

Made in the USA
Middletown, DE
27 March 2023

27791965R00038